METALLICA
ST. ANGER

Transcribed by Scott Schroedl

Album design by Metallica
Cover illustrations by Pushead
Album production design by Brad Klausen
Photography by Anton Corbijn
St. Anger illustrations by Matt Mahurin
James image by Matt Mahurin
Lars image by Forhelvede Productions
Kirk image by Matt Mahurin
Robert image by Pascal Brun & Comenius Röthlisberger
   (Team Switzerland)
Management by Q Prime Inc.

ISBN 1-57560-684-4

Visit our website at www.cherrylane.com

When you're able to brandish the kind of musical firepower that Metallica has unleashed for more than two decades—ten uncompromising albums, marking an unprecedented reign as *the greatest* hard rock band in history—you learn a thing or two about where to aim. But curiously enough, the making of their first studio album since 1997's *ReLoad*, the primal, raptorial, *St. Anger*, found Metallica not behind the turrets this time, but in the firing line itself.

The trials and tribulations leading up to *St. Anger* are well documented. The fissures in what the band members themselves describe as the well-oiled "Metallica machine" were beginning to show. Bassist Jason Newsted's nebulous exit from the group. James Hetfield's voluntary sojourn into rehab and much-longed-for sobriety. Public squabbles over the illegal downloading quagmire. All of these issues revealed the kind of seismic fault lines that even the Metallica juggernaut could not navigate—could not negotiate away.

At stake? Nothing less than the very existence of the band itself. Metallica's three principals, James Hetfield, Lars Ulrich, and Kirk Hammett, along with their frequent producer/collaborator Bob Rock, found themselves at the kind of crossroads worthy of the themes in many a Metallica song—the kind of foreboding scenario Ulrich and Hetfield could write in their sleep.

The irony was, if this was Metallica's oft-predicted *meltdown*, each member would have to face it in his own way. And from the inside out this time, without the Metallica heat shield to fend off all the bullshit that tends to calcify when you're a member of the most exclusive rock club in the world for 20-odd years. With James on an indefinite hiatus, the group admitted to becoming "professional speculators" themselves as to whether Metallica was headed for a rebirth or would wither away on life support.

"It has been a very interesting three years," Lars Ulrich begins, with atypical understatement. "A very different three years for us. Difficult, awkward. It's been a ride that's taken us to places inside ourselves, inside the band, inside the potential of human beings and the music and everything else that we could not imagine existed. But if you asked me then, I would say for the first time in my life with Metallica, I was starting to prepare myself that maybe the ride was over."

If it sounds like the tenets of a Herculean struggle, who else but Metallica to apply for the job. The result of the "ride" Lars refers to can indeed be found in the sweat and blood and grooves of *St. Anger*. From the album's crushing title song and its burnished heaps of magnified guitar and drums, to the colossal time and tempo changes of "Frantic," to the chugging slabs and staccato exchanges of the exalting confessional "My World," Metallica has once again, in the boldest strokes imaginable, made music its most viable currency.

The three band members, who gingerly refer to themselves as brothers—and mean it—emerged from the other side of their journey with their musical compass intact. S*t. Anger* is an album that invariably will draw comparisons to their best work, to Metallica's halcyon days, most notably their classic 1983 opus *Kill 'Em All*, and 1986's *Master of Puppets*. Monumental in scope, the new album also recalls—by its sheer willfulness—the group's 15-million selling masterpiece known as the Black album. But this is clearly a work that couldn't have been made 20 years ago. Not even a decade ago, though it fits the Metallica canon like a glove.

According to producer Rock (the Black album was his first collaboration with Metallica) *St. Anger* completes the circular creative cycle that only the greatest artists are able to sustain. "It's been my experience that only the big artists know how to achieve a goal in their career, like Metallica did with the Black album. Fewer still could have gone through what they experienced with all their personal journeys, throw away the rulebook, and try to capture the soul and truth of Metallica again. I think the real vision was to almost take them back to where they were first getting together, when three or four guys get together and say: This is the kind of music we like; let's write some songs."

For James, whose own personal quest may have been the tipping point for Metallica's inspirational sea change, the album was an

Kirk Hammett   Robert Trujillo   Lars Ulrich   James Hetfield

important step in their evolution not just as band members, but also as friends. "The early days of Metallica were about brotherhood, just survival mode, relying on each other and stuff. As the machine got bigger, you tend to forget about the friendship part and start worrying about where the machine is going. You get a little more protective, a little more isolated. Certain factors ignited the need to look inward again and just get to be friends. Now we're stronger than ever because we know what we're doing and we have experience on our side too."

Part of the familial equation the group had to deal with was the departure of Newsted and the search for a new bassist. Enter Rob Trujillo. A former member of Suicidal Tendencies and one of the masterminds behind the '90s cult band Infectious Grooves, the accomplished bassist has also played with none other than Ozzy Osbourne.

All three band members immediately hit it off with the respected Trujillo, and the hole in Metallica's musical armor was filled. Trujillo came aboard too late to appear on St. Anger. The band members did not seem to be in any rush to hire a bass player. Bob Rock, in addition to being the co-producer and co-songwriter on St. Anger, was considered the fourth member of the band. Bob even filled in (quite masterfully) at a few live events with the guys. But, as Metallica guitarist Kirk Hammett points out, Trujillo's chemistry with the band is undeniable. "From the first rehearsal Rob was just mind-blowing, because he had such a huge sound and he pulled with his fingers, which is very reminiscent of Cliff Burton, and we really liked that sound. He delivered on all fronts. He had a big sound and on top of that he's really a great, solid guy." Adds James: "He pounds. The power that comes through his fingers. He's a ball of energy and he's so calm and able and balanced. He's got great stuff to offer but his personality is just right. He's on fire, he's ready, he's plugged right into the strength of Metallica and helping it shine."

Another aspect of Metallica's rejuvenated approach on this album is Hammett's joining in on the lyric writing, territory previously exclusive to James and Lars. "At first I was like, I don't want anything to do with this; this is James' job. But Bob was very adamant. I

looked at James and I said, 'Well, how do I do this?' James said 'stream of consciousness.' I would scribble down some lines and James would single out the good ones. It was a great experience and I think it's all in line with the theme of the album, if there is an underlying theme, which is just being true to yourself and how important that is to the overall picture."

Which leads to what is sure to be another topic of discussion among Metallica-watchers when poring over the epic arrangements and knife-edged nuances of St. Anger. For a band that is in the throes of introspection, and in a larger sense, collective healing, they sure have laid down some motherfucking aggressive music. For hardcore fans who patiently waded through their all-covers release, 1998's Garage Inc., a spry homage to the songs that shaped their early career, and the symphonic wanderlust of S&M, a stirring experiment that showcased Metallica with noted producer/writer/arranger Michael Kamen and the San Francisco Symphony, St. Anger is a thirst-quencher. But one that offers nothing but fire this time around.

Lars says there was no conscious effort to make this album louder or longer. "I think the great thing about Metallica is that we can pretty much chart where we want to chart. Playing other people's material (like on Garage Inc.) was something we talked about for years. It was the music the band was basically founded on. With the symphony stuff we got a call from Michael Kamen who wanted to do it and the band was excited by the challenge—something Metallica has always embraced. "But now that we are back playing the stuff that people think is the purest, it is the most natural, it is the most effortless. The other thing I think we're challenging here is the perception most people have that in order for things to be really, really, energetic, they can only come from negative energy. Metallica was fueled by negative energy for 20 years. Now we've spent a lot of time working on ourselves and on our relationships, and we've turned that around. Now Metallica is fueled by positive energy that has manifested itself so it sounds like the album we've made."

Case in point: "Some Kind of Monster," with its bristling, time bomb refrain, and yet, under-neath, a hint of affirmation: "This is the voice of silence no more." You begin to understand the

complex dynamics required for a world-renowned construct like Metallica even to be able to conceive of an intensely personal triumph like St. Anger. For James the process obviously begins in a much quieter place than a recording studio. "It comes from us realizing the world doesn't revolve around Metallica. For me it began with "my name is James Hetfield." St. Anger means to me that now that we've found our serenity we're capable of making this monster of an album going full throttle all the time. Anger is an energy. It's a feeling. It's gotten a bad reputation, but it's what you do with it after that gives it its reputation. I could squeeze out sideways with rage and stuff the shit down, yet it can be such a source of strength. Metallica has always been about invading places where we don't belong. We just took down the barbed wire, that's all."

DISCOGRAPHY

Kill 'Em All	July 1983
Ride the Lightning	August 1984
Master of Puppets	February 1986
Garage Days Re-Revisited	August 1987
...And Justice for All	August 1988
Metallica	August 1991
Live Shit: Binge & Purge	December 1993
Load	June 1996
ReLoad	November 1997
Garage Inc.	November 1998
S&M	November 1999
St. Anger	June 2003

Metallica Web Site: www.metallica.com

Metallica Fan Club: www.metclub.com

Metallica Fan Club mailing address:

The Metallica Club
369-B Third St.
PMB #194
San Rafael, CA 94901

contents

6   frantic

12   st. anger

20   some kind of monster

29   dirty window

35   invisible kid

46   my world

57   shoot me again

66   sweet amber

72   the unnamed feeling

80   purify

86   all within my hands

95   drum notation legend

Editor's Note:

Because Metallica tune their guitars down a whole step for most songs on this album, the vocal lines in this folio sound a whole step lower than written. Exceptions are "Dirty Window," which sounds a half step lower, and "Invisible Kid," which sounds as written.

Lars Ulrich's drum kit includes two bass drums. For all fast bass drum passages, alternate between bass drums one and two.

FRANTIC

Words and Music by
James Hetfield, Lars Ulrich,
Kirk Hammett and Bob Rock

Verse

1. If I could have ___ my wast - ed days ___ back, would
worn out al - ways be - ing a - fraid, an

I use them ___ to get ___ back on ___ track, stop to warm ___ at kar -
end - less stream ___ of fear ___ that I've ___ made. Tread - ing wa - ter full ___

- mas burn - ing or look a - head ___ but keep ___ on turn - ing?
___ of wor - ry, this fran - tic, tick, ___ tick, talk ___ of hur - ry.

Do I have the strength to know how I'll go? ___ Can I find it in - side to

deal with what I should - n't know? Could I have ___ my wast - ed days ___ back? Would
Worn out al - ways be - ing a - fraid, an

End half-time feel

I use them ___ to get ___ back on ___ track?
end - less stream ___ of fear ___ that I've ___ made.

And I need to set my an - ger free.

And I need to

set my an - ger free, _____ ah! And I

need to set my an - ger free. _____

Interlude
Double-time feel

Set it free! _____

End double-time feel

Play 7 times

D.S.S. al Coda 2

18

19

SOME KIND OF MONSTER

Words and Music by
James Hetfield, Lars Ulrich,
Kirk Hammett and Bob Rock

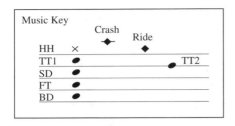

Intro

Moderately slow Rock ♩ = 108

*Play Ride on edge for washy sound throughout.
**Snares off throughout.

Double-time feel

End double-time feel

Verse

1. These are the eyes __ that can't __ see me, these are the hands __ that drop __ your trust.
3. This is the face __ that stones __ you cold, this is the mo - ment that needs __ to breathe.

These are the boots __ that kick __ you a - round, this is the tongue __ that speaks __ on the in - side.
These are the claws __ that scratch __ these wounds, this is the pain __ that nev - er leaves. __

These are the ears ___ that ring ___ with hate, this is the face ___ that - 'll nev - er change.
This is the tongue ___ that whips ___ you down, this is the bur - den of ev - 'ry man.

This is the fist ___ that grinds ___ you down,) this is the voice ___ of si - lence ___ no
These are the screams ___ that pierce ___ your skin,}

Interlude

more.

{ 1. *Voc. tacet*
{ 2. Yeah!   Yeah!

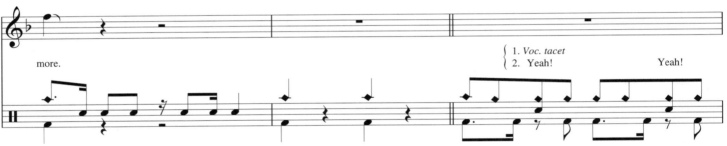

Yeah!   Yeah!   Yeah!   Yeah!   Yeah!   Yeah!

Verse

2. These are the legs ___ in cir - cles run, this is the beat - ing you'll nev - er know. ___
4. This is the test ___ of flesh and soul, this is the trap ___ that smells so good.

These are the lips ___ that taste ___ no free-dom, this is the feel ___ that's not ___ so safe.
This is the flood ___ that drains ___ these eyes, these are the looks ___ that chill ___ to the bone.

This is the face ___ you'll nev-er change, this is the god ___ that ain't ___ so pure.
These are the fears ___ that swing o-ver-head, these are the weights ___ that hold ___ you down.

This is the god ___ that is ___ not pure,) this is the voice ___ of si-lence ___ no
This is the end ___ that will nev-er end,)

more.

Pre-Chorus

We the peo-ple, _____

23

are we   the peo - ple?

We   the peo - ple, ___

are we   the peo - ple? ___

Chorus

Some kind ___ of mon - ster.

24

Some kind __ of mon - ster. _____ Some kind __ of

mon - ster.

2nd time, w/ Fill 1

This mon - ster lives.

Interlude

1.

Fill 1

Bridge

This is the cloud__ that swal - lows trust, this is the black__ that un - col - ors us.

This is the face__ that you__ hide from, this is the mask__ that comes__ un - done.__

(Om - i - nous,__ I'm____ in us. Om - i - nous,__ I'm____ in us.

Om - i - nous,__ I'm____ in us. Om - i - nous,__ I'm____ in us.)

This is the cloud that swallows trust, this is the black that uncolors us.

This is the face that you hide from, this is the mask that comes undone.

(Ominous, I'm in us. Ominous, I'm in us.

Ominous, I'm in us. Ominous, I'm in us.)

Interlude

Are we the peo - ple? _____

Chorus

Some kind _ of mon - ster. Some kind _ of

mon - ster. _____ Some kind _ of mon - ster. _____ This mon - ster lives. _____

Outro

28

DIRTY WINDOW

Words and Music by
James Hetfield, Lars Ulrich,
Kirk Hammett and Bob Rock

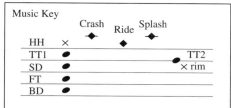

It _____ looks dif - f'rent, _____ so dif - f'rent _____ than what you see. _____
This win - dow, clean in - side, dirt - y on the out.

Pro - ject - ing judg - ment on the world. _____
I'm look - ing dif - fer - ent than me. _____

End double-time feel

This house is clean, ba - by; _____ this house is clean.

Pre-Chorus
Double-time feel

Am I who I think I am? _____ Am _____ I who I think I am? _____

*Play Ride on edge for washy sound.

To Coda ⊕ | 1.

| 2.

Interlude

32

Outro

Bkgd. Voc.: w/ Voc. Fig. 1 (4 times)

I _____ drink from ___ the cup of ___ de - ni - al. _____

I'm _____ judg - ing ___ the world from ___ my

1. throne. _____   **2.** throne. _____

Yeah!

INVISIBLE KID

Words and Music by
James Hetfield, Lars Ulrich,
Kirk Hammett and Bob Rock

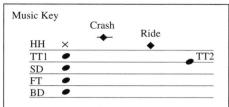

Intro

Moderately fast Rock ♩ = 164

*Snares off throughout

**Play Ride on edge for washy sound throughout.

Interlude

way.   In - to   dis -   tance

let   me   fade.   I'm   o -

2nd & 3rd times, Bkgd. Voc.: w/ Voc. Fig. 1

kay,   just   go   a -   way.

I'm   o - kay,   but   please   don't

stray   too   far.

Voc. Fig. 1

(I'm   o - kay.   I'm...   But

please   don't   stray   too   far.)

Play 3 times

Slower ♩ = 148

Ooh.

Bridge

Ooh, _____ what a good ___ boy ___ you are, ___
Ooh, _____ ooh, un - plug - ging from ___ it all, ___ in -

out of the way ___ and you kept to your - self. ___
vis - i - ble kid ___ floats a - lone in his ___ room. ___

Ooh, _____ can't you see that he's ___ not here? ___
Ooh, _____ what a qui - et boy ___ you are. ___

He does -n't want_____ the at - ten - tion you____ give. _____
He looks so calm____ float - ing 'round____

_____ and a - round____ in him - self. _____

Interlude
Tempo I

Play 3 times

44

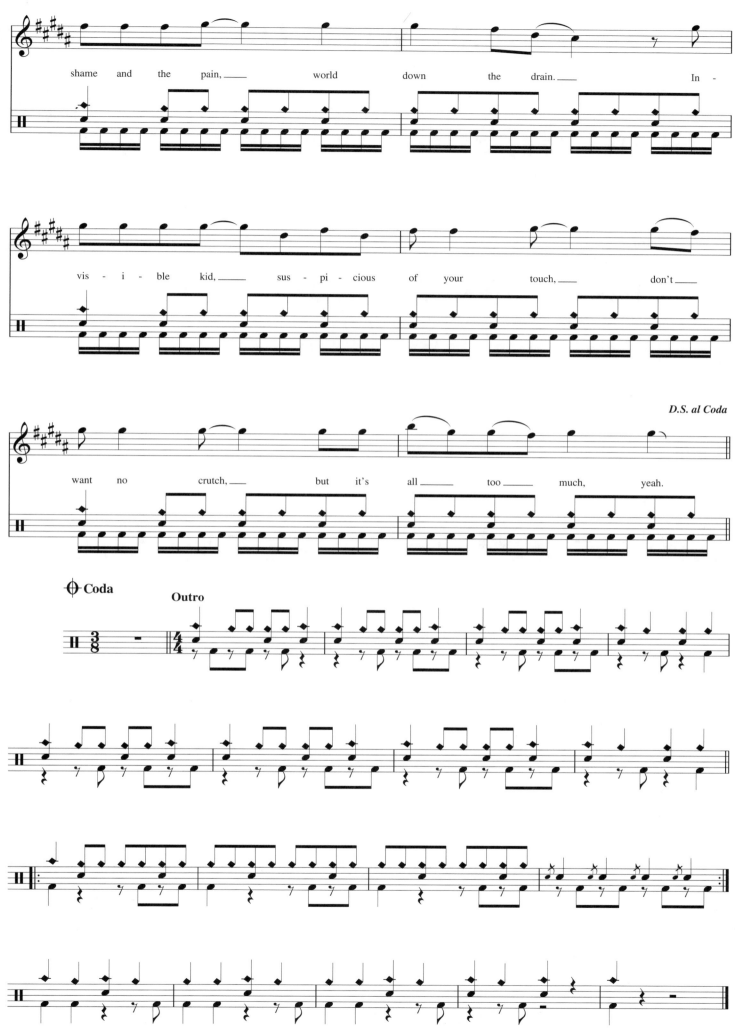

shame and the pain, _____ world down the drain. _____ In -

vis - i - ble kid, _____ sus - pi - cious of your touch, _____ don't _____

D.S. al Coda

want no crutch, _____ but it's all _____ too _____ much, yeah.

Coda

Outro

45

MY WORLD

Words and Music by
James Hetfield, Lars Ulrich,
Kirk Hammett and Bob Rock

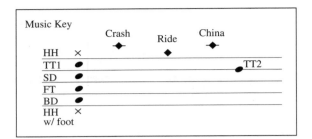

Chorus

Half-time feel

48

I'm out of my head, _____ out of my head. _____

Get 'em out of my head, _____ out of my head. _____

Get 'em out! Ah, yeah. *Whispered:* Suck - er. __

End half-time feel

Verse

3. Who's in charge _ of my head to - day? _____

Half-time feel

End half-time feel

Verse

Dancin' devils in angels' way. It's my time now. It's my time now. It's my time. Yeah, it's my time.

4. Look out, mother-fuck-ers, here I come. I'm gonna make my head my home. The sons-of-bitches try'n' to take my head. Try'n' to

50

Chorus

51

Interlude

End half-time feel

Play 3 times

Play 4 times

Whispered: Not on - ly

China

do I not know ___ the an - swer, I don't ___ e -

ven know what the ___ ques - tion is.

China

52

53

54

55

SHOOT ME AGAIN

Words and Music by
James Hetfield, Lars Ulrich,
Kirk Hammett and Bob Rock

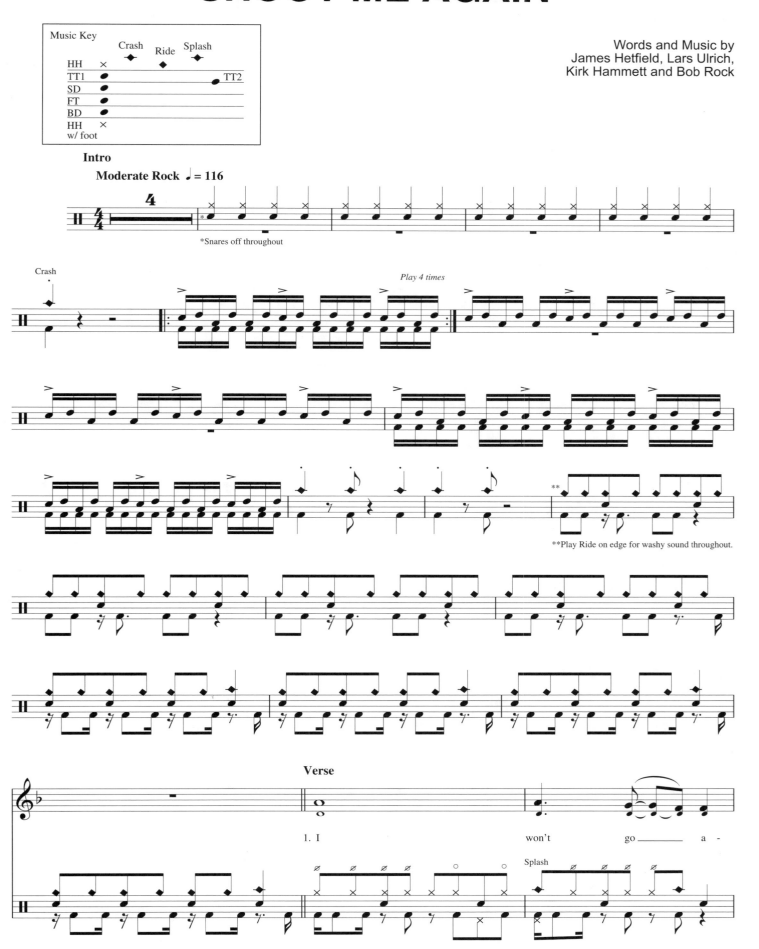

way, _____ ah! Right, _____

right   here _____ I'll   stay. _____

Interlude

Verse

2. Stand   si - lent _____ in

flames. _____   Stand _____

tall   till _____ it   fades. _____

Chorus

All the shots___ I take _____ I spit back at ___ you. _____

_____ All the shit___ you fake _____ comes

back to haunt___ you. _____ All the shots...___

All the shots...___ { All the shots___ I take, _____ } what
{ All the shots___ I take, _____ hey, }

2nd time, Bkgd. Voc.: w/ Voc. Fig. 1

dif - f'rence did ___ I _____ make? _____ All the shots___ I take, ___

Voc. Fig. 1

(What dif - f'rence did I make?)

60

I spit back at ___ you. ___ Oh, ___ whoa,

Interlude

oh, ah!

To Coda ⊕ **Verse**

3. I won't go ___ a-
Splash

way, ___ Right, ___
(with a bul-let in my back.
Crash

right ___ here ___ I'll stay ___
with a bul-let in my back.)
Splash   Crash

Interlude

Shoot me.   Shoot me.   Mm, shoot me.
(Take a shot.   Take a shot.   Take a shot.

61

Bridge

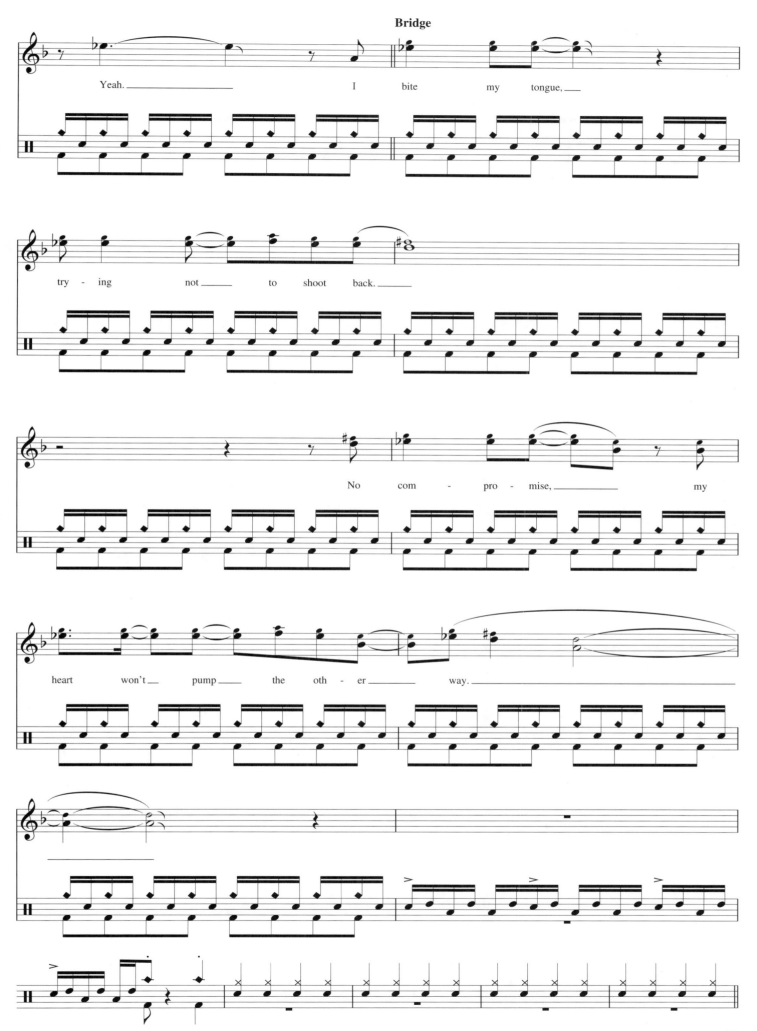

Yeah. _____ I bite my tongue, _____ try - ing not _____ to shoot back. _____ No com - pro - mise, _____ my heart won't _____ pump _____ the oth - er _____ way. _____

63

Wake the sleep - ing gi - ant, __ wake the beast. Wake the sleep - ing dog, no, let him sleep.
(No!)

Bite my tongue, __ try - ing not __ to shoot back.

Chorus

All the shots __ I take __

I spit back at __ you, __

yeah. __ All the shit __ you fake __

comes back to haunt __ you, __

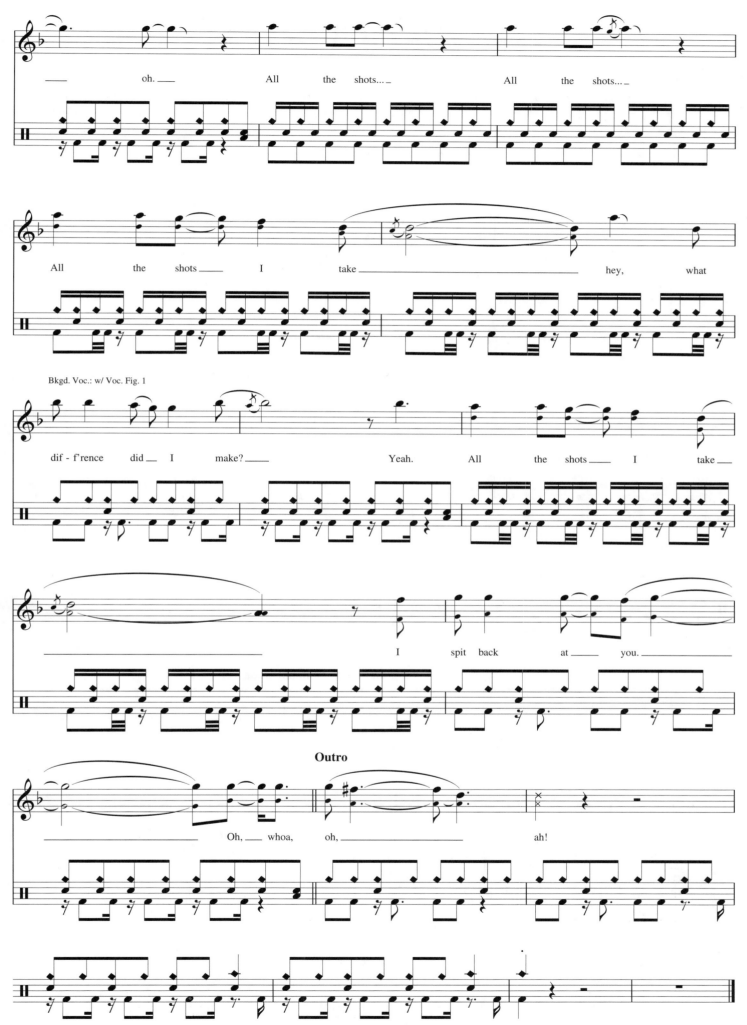

SWEET AMBER

Words and Music by
James Hetfield, Lars Ulrich,
Kirk Hammett and Bob Rock

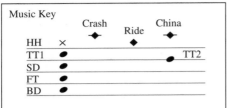

*Snares off throughout

**Play Ride on edge for washy sound throughout.

D.S. al Coda 1

End double-time feel

Coda 1

get?

Bridge

holds   the   pen _____   that   spells _____   the   end. _____   She   trac -

She

70

THE UNNAMED FEELING

Words and Music by
James Hetfield, Lars Ulrich,
Kirk Hammett and Bob Rock

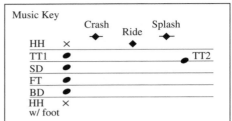

Intro

Moderately fast Rock ♩ = 144

*Snares off throughout

Whispered: (Been here be - fore. Been here be - fore.)

**Play Ride on edge for washy sound throughout.

(Been here be - fore. Been here be - fore.)

1. Been here be - fore, ___ could - n't say I liked ___ it. Yeah,
fran - tic in ___ your sooth - ing arms, ___ I

do I start ___ writ - ing all this down? ___ Just
can - not sleep ___ in this down - filled world. ___ I've found

let me plug ___ you in - to my ___ world. Can't ya help ___ me be
safe - ty in ___ this lone - li - ness, ___ but I can - not stand ___ it an -

___ un - cra - zy? ___ Name this for ___ me, heat ___
- y - more. ___ Cross my heart, ___ hope not ___

___ the cold ___ air. Take the chill ___ off ___ of ___ my life. ___ And
___ to die. ___ Swal - low e - vil, ___ ride ___ the sky. ___

if I could ___ I'd turn ___ my eyes ___ to look in - side ___ to see ___
Lose my - self ___ in a crowd - ed room. ___ You fool, you fool, ___ it - 'll be ___

And then the un - named feel - ing, _____ it

takes me _____ a - way, _____ it takes me... _____

Chorus

Then the un - named _____ feel - ing, it comes _____ a - live,

_____ yeah, _____ yeah. Then the un - named _____ feel - ing _____

takes me _____ a - way, _____ yeah, takes me _____ a - way, _

Interlude

Play 3 times

_____ ah!

Chorus

2nd time, w/ Fill 1

Then the un - named feel - ing, it
Then I wait for this train, my toes are

comes a - live, yeah, yeah.
o - ver the line, yeah.
Then the

Fill 1

un - named feel - ing treats me this way.

takes me a - way, yeah,

Outro-Chorus

takes me a - way, ah! Then the un - named feel -

- ing, it comes a - live.

Then the un - named feel - ing

takes me a - way.

Splash

PURIFY

Words and Music by
James Hetfield, Lars Ulrich,
Kirk Hammett and Bob Rock

Verse

2. Truth and dare, peel - ing back the skin. Ac - id wash, ghost white, ul - tra clean wan - na - be skel - e - ton. Clear eyes, dia - mond eyes.

D.S. al Coda 1

Strip the past of mine, my sweet tur - pen -

Coda 1

Mm, _____ ah, ha, ha, ha, ha, ha, ha!

ALL WITHIN MY HANDS

Words and Music by
James Hetfield, Lars Ulrich,
Kirk Hammett and Bob Rock

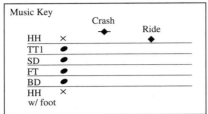

*Snares off throughout

**Play Ride on edge for washy sound throughout, except where otherwise indicated.

***Play Ride w/ tip of stick on surface (next 16 meas.).

All with - in

my hands.

Verse

1., 3. All with - in _____ my hands. _____ { Squeeze it in, _____ Take your fear, _____

_____ crush it down. _____ } _____ pump me up. _____

All with - in _____ my hands. _____ { Hold it dear, _____ Let you run, _____

_____ hold it, suf - fo - cate. _____ _____ then I pull _____ your _____ leash. _____

Interlude

Ah, _____

All _____ with -

Verse

2., 4. All with - in my hands.

Love to death,
Un - der thumb,

smack you 'round and 'round and...
un - der to my - self.

All with - in my hands. Be - ware.

88

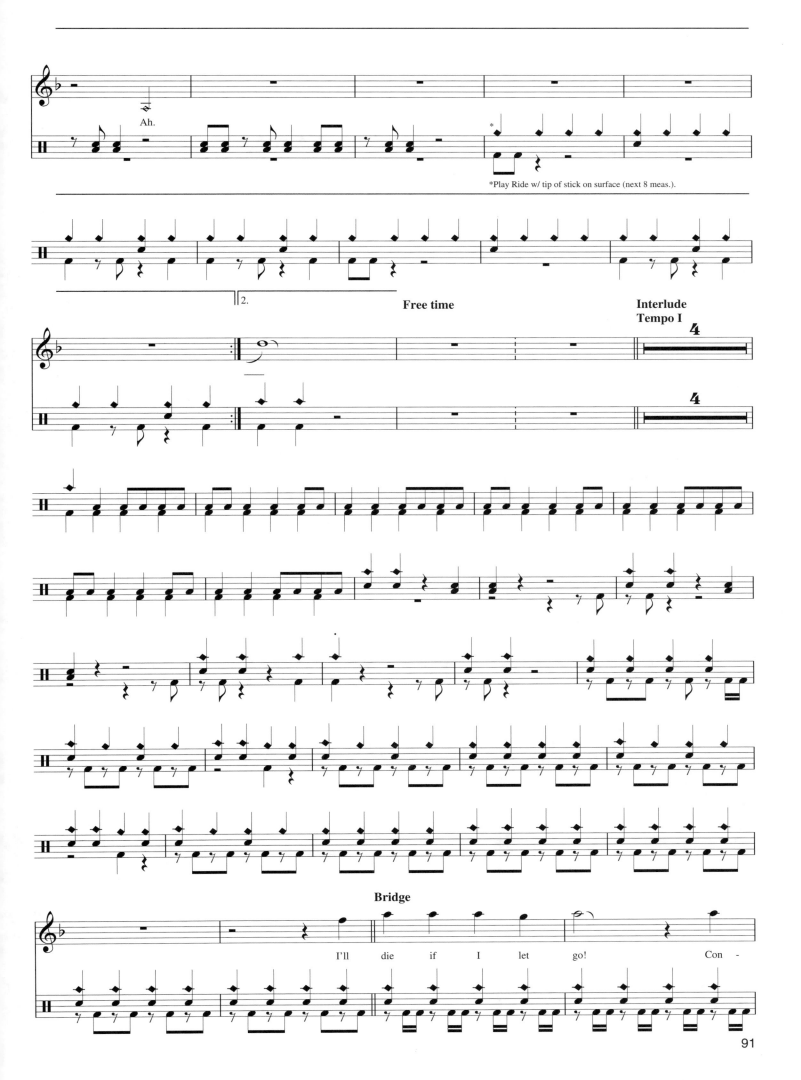

Ah.

*Play Ride w/ tip of stick on surface (next 8 meas.).

2.

Free time

Interlude
Tempo I

4

4

Bridge

I'll   die   if   I   let   go!   Con -

D.S. al Coda

Ah!

Love   is   con - trol!

Coda
Tempo I

Outro

Kill,   kill,   kill,   kill,   kill!   Kill,   kill,   kill,

kill,   kill!   Kill,   kill,   kill,

kill,   kill!

Kill, ____ kill,

kill,   kill, ____ kill! ____

Kill,   kill,   kill,

kill,   kill!   Kill!   Kill! ____

Slower   **A Tempo**

Kill!

Kill,   kill,   kill,

kill! ____

Kill,   kill,   kill,

Half time ♩ = 108
Freely

Play 3 times

kill,   kill!   Kill!

(Sing 1st time only)

94

HI-HAT

OPEN AND CLOSED HI-HAT: Strike the open hi-hat on notes labeled with an *o*. Strike the closed hi-hat on unlabeled notes.

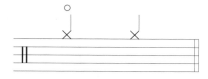

HI-HAT WITH FOOT: Clap hi-hat cymbals together with foot pedal.

HI-HAT WITH SLUR: The open hi-hat is struck and then closed with the foot on the beat indicated by the hi-hat w/foot notation below, creating a *shoop* sound.

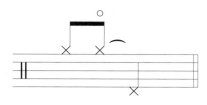

HI-HAT BARK: The open hi-hat is struck and is immediately, almost simultaneously closed so that the *shoop* sound is severely clipped.

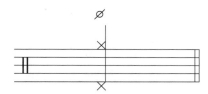

CYMBALS

CHOKE: Hit the crash cymbal and catch it immediately with the other hand, producing a short, choked crash sound.

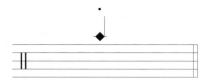

BELL OF CYMBAL: Hit the cymbal near the center, directly on the cup or bell portion.

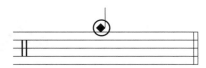

CYMBAL ROLL: Play a roll on the cymbal rapidly enough to produce a sustained, uninterrupted *shhh* sound lasting for the number of beats indicated.

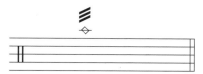

DRUMS

CROSS STICK: Anchor the tip end of the stick on the snare drum skin at the eight o'clock position, two to three inches from the rim. Then raise and lower the butt end, striking the rim at the two o'clock position, producing a clicky, woodblock-type sound.

FLAM: Hit the drum with both sticks, one slightly after the other, producing a single, thick-sounding note.

RUFF: Play the grace notes rapidly and as close to the principal note as possible. The grace notes are unaccented and should be played slightly before the beat. The principal note is accented and played directly on the beat.

CLOSED ROLL: Play a roll on the snare drum creating a sustained, uninterrupted *tshhh* sound lasting for the duration of the rhythm indicated and with no break between the two tied notes.